CITIES OF THE WORLD

RIO DE JANEIRO

BY DEBORAH KENT

CHILDREN'S PRESS®
A Division of Grolier Publishing
New York London Hong Kong Sydney
Danbury, Connecticut

CONSULTANTS

Miriam Ayres, Ph.D.
Lecturer, Department of Spanish and Portuguese
New York University

Monica Reis
Native of Rio de Janeiro
Teacher of Portuguese, Berlitz International, New York

Project Editor: Downing Publishing Services
Design Director: Karen Kohn & Associates
Photo Researcher: Jan Izzo

Library of Congress Cataloging-in-Publication Data
Kent, Deborah.
    Rio de Janeiro / Deborah Kent.
      p. cm. — (Cities of the world)
    Summary: Provides a physical description and history, along with a discussion of the people
and customs, of the second largest city in Brazil.
    ISBN 0-516-00353-4
    1. Rio de Janeiro (Brazil)—Juvenile literature. [l. Rio de Janeiro (Brazil)]
I. Title. II. Series: Cities of the world (New York, N.Y.)
F2646.K46 1996   95-36157
981'.53—dc20   CIP
                                                AC

TABLE OF CONTENTS

MOUNTAIN

Every half hour throughout the day, visitors to Rio de Janeiro pile into the tiny, rattling cars of a cogwheel train and climb the mountain known as Corcovado. In places, the mountainside is so steep that the train seems ready to tumble backward into the bay far below. Somehow, the string of cars clings to the twisting track. It crawls steadily upward until it can go no farther. At last, the passengers clamber out and continue their journey on foot. They mount a flight of uneven stone steps to their final destination, the magnificent statue of Jesus Christ the Redeemer that overlooks the city.

Corcovado (koh-koh-VAH-doo)

The white concrete statue of Jesus Christ the Redeemer stands on top of the mountain known as Corcovado. The statue itself towers 120 feet tall, as high as a 12-story building. It weighs 700 tons. One hand alone weighs 8 tons. The mighty arms spread wide, giving the statue the form of a cross.

From the platform at the foot of the statue, visitors have a stunning view of the city. Flanked by gleaming glass-and-steel skyscrapers, Guanabara Bay sparkles like a polished stone. Endless beaches stretch away into the distance. Busy streets thread their way among rugged mountains green with rain forests.

Rio de Janeiro is the second largest city in Brazil. It is a bustling center of culture, business, and entertainment. The city is long and narrow, stretching some 15 miles along Brazil's Atlantic coast. Throngs of people fill the city, from the desperately poor to some of the wealthiest in all of Latin America.

The people of Rio love anything that is modern and new. A building is considered old if it has stood for more than a decade. Each year, Rio reaches out to engulf more and more of the surrounding rain forest. Yet its development is held in check by natural barriers. Rio is squeezed between the mountains on one side and the ocean on the other. Despite its passion for growth, the city must respect the forces of nature.

From the summit of Corcovado, the roar of traffic cannot be heard. The shouts of children and the cries of street vendors are lost in the wind. Like a city in a fairy tale, Rio shines below, full of magic and mystery.

This aerial picture shows the beautiful city of Rio as it looks from Corcovado.

Foreigners and even other Brazilians sometimes complain that the people of Rio are lazy. "It's not that we don't work—we do," insists Augusto Rodrigues, a leading Rio artist. "It's just that we don't want to." Cariocas love singing, dancing, and lounging on the beach. They work when they must, but almost any excuse is good enough for throwing a party. The term *carioca*, referring to a citizen of Rio, comes from an Indian word meaning "house of the white man."

In terms of ethnic background, religion, and class, the people of Rio span a wide range. Yet they all have a reputation for their unquenchable love of fun.

Augusto Rodrigues (OW-GOO-STOO HOH-DREE-GEHZ)
carioca (KAH-REE-OH-KAH)

RIO, HIGH AND LOW

Most bathers at Rio's beaches splash
in the shallows near the shore.

On any day of the year, Rio's Copacabana Beach is dense with people. Joggers pound along the strip of sand closest to the street. They are determined to keep their bodies lithe and beautiful. Despite the blazing sun, lively games of volleyball, tennis, and soccer are always in full swing. Nearer to the sea, men and women sprawl on beach towels. Children build castles in the sand. The crashing breakers are a challenge to even the strongest swimmer. Most people merely splash in the shallows to cool off. The beach is not really meant for swimming. It is a place where people go to enjoy the sun, to laugh and play, to be admired, and to admire one another.

Copacabana (KOH-PAH-KAH-BAH-NAH)
Ipanema (EE-PAH-NAY-MAH)
Barra da Tijuca (BAH-HAH DAH CHEE-ZHOO-KAH)

Rio's beaches and expensive high-rise apartments stretch along the southern edge of the city.

Copacabana, Ipanema, and Barra da Tijuca are among the most famous beaches in the world. They stretch along Rio's southern edge. Along the adjoining avenue rise exclusive modern high-rise apartments and condominiums. Beach property is among the most expensive on earth.

Wealthy business executives, politicians, movie stars, and sports figures make their homes here. Rugged mountain peaks separate this South Zone from the rest of Rio. It is connected to the central part of the city by tunnels that have been drilled through the mountains.

This young man is delivering cold slices of watermelon to sunbathers on Ipanema Beach.

Until recently, inflation in Brazil was among the highest in the world. Prices constantly rose, as much as 40 percent a year. After the election of President Fernando Henrique Cardoso in 1994, inflation nearly ceased as a problem. Wages for most workers are pitifully low, however. A Rio laborer would have to work for 300 years to afford a condo at Copacabana.

Each year, thousands of people pour into Rio from rural parts of Brazil. They are desperate for work, hoping for a chance to improve their lives. Instead, most of them find hopeless poverty.

About one-quarter of all Cariocas live in the city's *favelas*, or "vertical slums." The favelas are shantytowns that cling to the sides of Rio's many hills. People throw together tiny houses. They use any materials that come to hand—scraps of lumber, sheets of tin or plastic, and even cardboard boxes. Whole families—grandparents, parents, aunts and uncles, and children—crowd together into one or two rooms.

In most favelas, homes have no telephones, electricity, or running water. No trucks come around to collect the garbage. Some people claim they would rather live near the bottom of the hill, close to public faucets where they can fill a pail with water. When it rains, however,

This mother and her child live in one of Rio's many shantytowns, or favelas.

Two shantytown children sitting on a doorstep

stinking trash slithers down the hillside to pile up at their doors. Given a choice, many people prefer to live at the top of the hill, despite the long climb with heavy water buckets. The rain carries the garbage away from the houses at the top.

Because Rio is blighted by poverty, crime in the city is very high. Police corruption makes the situation even worse. Brazil has no official death penalty, but the police often take justice into their own hands. In 1994, police at a Rio mall seized a suspected shoplifter, dragged him into a corner, and executed him on the spot. A TV cameraman who happened to be nearby caught the grisly event on film. It aired on national television.

No one knows how many homeless children wander Rio's streets. They survive by begging, stealing, dealing drugs, or working as prostitutes. As one Rio social worker put it, "The kids are living under conditions of civil war, and in war all is fair, right?"

Many of the thrown-together shacks in Rio's favelas have been replaced with brick and concrete houses. This favela is on a bluff called Morro de Babilonia.

favela (FAH-VEH-LAH)

RIO'S ETHNIC MOSAIC

Some Cariocas can trace their ancestry back to the Portuguese colonists who came in the 1500s. Portuguese immigrants continued to arrive in Rio through the twentieth century. In the late 1800s and early 1900s, many Italians, Austrians, and Germans also came to Rio.

People of African ancestry make up about 30 percent of Rio's population. Persons of mixed African and European heritage are known as *mulatos*. In skin color, the people of Rio range from ivory white to darkest mahogany.

Much of Rio's character today has an African flavor. The city's music and dance grew from West African traditions. Pervading the atmosphere on every level of Rio society, there is *macumba*, the spiritist religion.

mulato (MOO-LAH-TOO)
macumba (MAH-KOOM-BAH)

As the pictures on these pages show, the skin color of Rio residents ranges from ivory white to darkest mahogany. This reflects the city's various racial mixes of Africans, European immigrants, and Native Americans.

POTIONS
AND
PRIESTS

As the statue of Christ the Redeemer suggests, Rio de Janeiro is a Roman Catholic city. Catholic priests were among the first Europeans to reach Guanabara Bay. With threats and promises, they baptized as many Indians as they could. Later, they turned to the colony's African slaves as a new source of converts.

The slaves took readily to Christianity—not that they had much choice in the matter. The priests taught them about an all-powerful, all-knowing God whose Son cared for humankind. The Christian God and his Son were flanked by a large supporting cast of saints. Satan lurked in the shadows, luring the unwary into evil. In many ways, these Christian figures resembled the gods and goddesses that the West Africans brought with them to the New World. The God of the priests was not unlike Olorun, the

Olorun (OH-LOH-ROONGH)
Ioruba (EE-YOH-ROO-BAH)
orixás (OH-REE-SHAHS)
Iemanjá (YEH-MAHN-ZHAH)
Oxossi (OH-SHOH-SEE)
exus (EH-CHOO)

chief god of the Ioruba people. Olorun was so mighty that human beings could not deal with him directly. Instead, they reached him through a gallery of lesser gods, or *orixás*. The greatest of these orixás was Gala, who somewhat resembled Jesus Christ. Iemanjá was the goddess of the sea and mother of the orixás. She was identified with Mary, the Mother of Jesus. The lesser orixás matched many of the Christian saints. Ogun, god of war, became St. George, who once killed a dragon. Oxossi, god of hunting, turned into St. Sebastian, who was shot to death with arrows. The Africans easily grasped the concept of Satan. They had their own *exus*, or powerful demonic spirits.

The dome of Rio's Candelária church was completed in 1877.

Outwardly, the African Brazilians were devout Christians. But they continued to worship their old gods and carry out the rituals of their own ancient religion. Many of these rituals and beliefs flourish in Rio to this day.

When they are sick or in trouble, Cariocas usually pray to Christ and the saints for help. But many loyal Catholics also turn to the orixás. On beaches or roadsides, they burn votive candles and place offerings of rum and cigarettes for the spirits. In both rich and poor neighborhoods, shops sell herbal love potions, jaguar's teeth, bat's wings, and dried toads. They are used in special ceremonies. These religious practices are often referred to as macumba, or spiritism.

People who follow spiritism believe that the souls of the dead can affect the world of the living. These souls, or spirits, can be called on for acts of mercy or vengeance. At spiritist temples or centers, carefully trained priests and priestesses call the spirits from the land beyond death. The spirit enters the body of a human medium. The medium goes into a trance and speaks with the spirit's voice.

Many Cariocas who consider themselves Roman Catholics also carry out the ancient rituals of spiritism. This woman is taking part in a spiritist ceremony. She may also attend mass at the Roman Catholic cathedral pictured below.

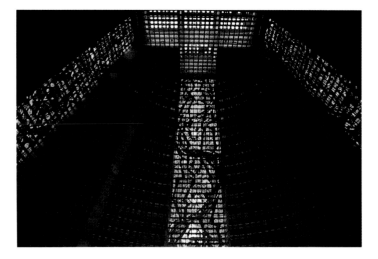

The interior of a modern Roman Catholic cathedral in Rio

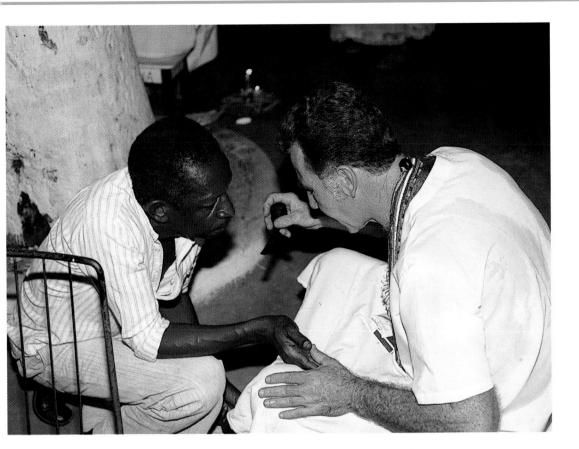

José Arigó

When they are ill, some Cariocas go to spiritist healers rather than medical doctors. One such healer is José Arigó. Arigó rose to international fame during the 1950s. Using kitchen knives and scissors that he kept in an old tin can, he performed hundreds of operations without anesthesia. His patients reported no discomfort. Doctors were amazed by his success, which scientists cannot explain to this day.

Brazilian spiritism has several branches. In Rio, the most widely practiced form is called Umbanda. Umbanda combines African spiritism with the rites of a spiritual movement that arose in France during the nineteenth century. The resulting blend is uniquely Brazilian. It is a medley of solemn rituals and vibrant festivals designed to heal the body and give wings to the soul.

Umbanda (OOM-BAHN-DAH)
José Arigó (ZHOH-ZEH AH-REE-GOH)

S.SEBASTIEN

BAY

E. Capucins
F. Cathedrale
G. Fort

B

In 1492, Christopher Columbus landed on a string of tiny islands now known as the West Indies. Not until his third voyage did he manage to find the continent of South America. Even then, he missed the land that is present-day Brazil. It was Pedro Alvares Cabral, a captain from the seafaring nation of Portugal, who became the first European to set foot on the Brazilian coast. In 1500, Cabral claimed Brazil for the Portuguese crown.

Pedro Alvares Cabral (PAY-DROH AHL-VAH-RAYS KAH-BRAHL)

THE EMPEROR'S GOLDEN AGE

O n March 1, 1565, a group of Portuguese soldiers arrived on the shore of Guanabara Bay. Their leader, Estácio de Sá, had instructions from Portugal. He was to establish a colony on the bay, and to drive out Portugal's enemies once and for all. Estácio de Sá and his men built a small mud-walled fort. It was surrounded by a moat for added protection. They christened the settlement São Sebastião do Rio de Janeiro, in tribute to Portugal's king, Dom Sebastião I. In the king's honor, they set up a statue of St. Sebastian in a tiny thatched chapel.

For more than six decades, the nations of western Europe had been grabbing up land in the New World. Portugal claimed the long Brazilian coast and the unexplored territory farther inland. French colonists, however, had built a fort on an island in Guanabara Bay. They challenged Portuguese rule.

Portuguese soldier Estácio de Sá and his men founded São Sebastião do Rio de Janeiro.

Estácio de Sá (EH-STAH-SEE-OH GEE SAH)
São Sebastião (SOW SE-BAH-STEE-OW)
Dom Sebastião (DONGH SE-BAH-STEE-OW)
Bahia (BY-EE-AH)
Tamoio (TAH-MOY-OOH)

The Native American Tamoio lived a simple life before the Portuguese arrived. They hunted and fished and lived off the land.

Two years passed before Estácio de Sá could carry out his orders from the homeland. At last, reinforcements arrived from Bahia, a Portuguese settlement to the north. On January 20, 1567, de Sá led a bold attack against the French fort. Riding bravely at the head of his troops, he flung himself against the French and their Indian allies. A poisoned arrow struck him in the face. A few weeks later, he died from his wound. Despite their fallen leader, the Portuguese were victorious. Today, January 20 is celebrated as a holiday in the city of Rio de Janeiro.

The Tamoio were the natives of the region. At first, they greeted the newcomers warmly. But the Portuguese tried to use the Tamoio as slaves. Tens of thousands of Tamoio died of smallpox and other diseases brought to the New World by the Europeans. Those who survived fled to the forests farther inland.

23

The Gloria Church, built in the 1700s, overlooks Guanabara Bay.

For two centuries after Estácio de Sá's victory, Rio flourished as a seaport. At first, ships at Rio's wharves took on cargoes of sugar bound for the Old World. Later, when gold was discovered, ships sailed out of Rio laden with treasure.

Many hands were needed to work the mines and sugar plantations. The Portuguese colonists looked to Africa for a cheap labor supply. About 600,000 Africans were shipped to Brazil during the 1600s. The number swelled to 2 million in the century that followed. By 1800, people of African descent outnumbered European settlers. For millions of African slaves, Rio's waterfront was the first glimpse of a new land.

Guanabara Bay bristled with the masts of slave ships and trading vessels. Then, in 1807, the royal fleet of Portugal sailed into the harbor. Portugal's prince regent, Dom João, was fleeing Napoleon Bonaparte, who had conquered Portugal as well as most of the rest of Europe.

Dom João (left) took refuge in Brazil. As King João VI, he set up his royal court in Rio. In 1822, King João's son Pedro I declared Brazil an independent nation, with himself as emperor. With Rio as its capital, Brazil became a European-style kingdom.

Dom João (DONGH ZHOW)
João VI (ZHOW SEHS-TOO)

Below: Slaves laboring in Brazil during the 1850s as an overseer looks on

Emperor Pedro II reigned over Brazil's golden age.

Brazil made great strides under Emperor Pedro II, who took the throne when he was only fourteen years old. Pedro II enjoyed a peaceful reign for nearly half a century, from 1840 to 1889. This era is often regarded as Brazil's golden age. It was a time of growth and prosperity.

Pedro II was fascinated by scientific discoveries. He was the first Brazilian ever to have his photograph taken or to speak on a telephone. He installed a system of mule-drawn trolleys in Rio. Steam locomotives linked the capital with outlying suburbs. International trade expanded, and Brazil's first transatlantic cable linked Rio with Europe.

As the emperor's reign went on, slavery was abolished in the United States and in the rest of Latin America. The sugar and coffee planters of Brazil, however, were unwilling to give up their slave labor. Princess Isabel, the daughter of Pedro II, worked hard for the antislavery cause in her

When Princess Isabel (above) abolished slavery in 1888, former slaves became part of everyday society (left).

Isabel (EE-ZAH-BAYL)
Lei Aurea (LAY OW-REE-AH)

country. In 1888, while her father was away, she signed the *Lei Aurea*, or Golden Law. It ended slavery forever in Brazil. Brazil was the last country in the New World to make slavery illegal.

"You have redeemed a race and lost a crown," one planter told the princess. The following year, Pedro II was overthrown by his political enemies. For the first time in its history, Brazil became a republic, with Rio de Janeiro as its capital.

THE CITY THAT GREW AND GREW

Some cities become monuments to their history. They carefully preserve old houses, churches, and markets as cherished mementos of the past. Rio de Janeiro has kept some of its oldest landmarks intact. But it is a city that honors change more than history. Cariocas hunger for anything that is newer, bigger, and faster than what they had before.

During the twentieth century, Rio's old houses tumbled as superhighways cut across the city. Once-quiet streets became broad avenues choked with traffic. Towering office buildings rose, only to be torn down to make room for buildings that soared even higher.

As the years passed, Rio spread over hillsides, around mountains, and along beaches up and down the coast. Yet the interior of Brazil remained a vast region of untouched rain forest. In 1956, Brazil's president, Juscelino Kubitschek, decided to build a new capital in the jungle. The new city, Brasília, was created in little more than three years. On April 21, 1960, Brasília became the official seat of government.

Dozens of government bureaus moved from Rio to Brasília. But the new capital could not really compete with Rio. Many government workers spend their weekdays in Brasília, but rush back to Rio every Friday night. Rio has the stores, the music, the beaches, and the excitement they crave. For most Cariocas, the sense of excitement is forever bound up with the fiercely modern city they call home.

Even though government workers must spend weekdays in Brasília, they go "home" to Rio (right) on the weekends.

Brasília (BRAH-ZEEL-YAH)

President Kubitschek accepted the key to Brasília on April 21, 1960, even though much of the new capital was still under construction.

Avenida Atlântica

Along Avenida Atlântica and many of Rio's other major thoroughfares, the sidewalks are made of mosaic tiles with a distinct wavy pattern. When Cariocas are late for an appointment, they sometimes blame the tiles. They joke that the swirling patterns on the sidewalks make it impossible for them to walk in a straight line.

Avenida Atlântica (AH-VAY-NEE-DAH AHT-LAHN-TEE-KAH)

CELEBRATION!

The people of Rio are famous the world over for knowing how to have a good time. They fling themselves into festivals, parades, and games. African and European traditions merge when Cariocas gather in celebration.

THE GODDESS OF THE SEA

On New Year's Eve, thousands of people stream toward Copacabana, Ipanema, and Rio's other beaches. They are all dressed in white—men and women, young and old, the very rich and the poorest of the poor. By 10 P.M. they are hard at work, arranging candles and bouquets of flowers on the sand. Some unfold lacy tablecloths and cover them with bright ribbons, lipsticks, combs, and necklaces. All of these things are gifts for Iemanjá, the goddess of the sea.

The new year is a fresh beginning, a time of hope. Spiritists in Rio and other parts of Brazil believe that Iemanjá will grant their wishes for the coming year if they please her with their offerings. As midnight approaches, the beach is alight with winking candles. People sing and dance, calling the goddess to join them.

At the stroke of midnight, the beach erupts into a din of bells and drums, sirens and firecrackers. Some people rush into the water and try to hurl their gifts beyond the breakers. Others wait on the sand for the rising tide to carry their offerings out to sea. It is a bad omen if the waves throw a gift back onto the beach. But if the sea carries a gift away, Iemanjá has accepted it gladly, and all will be well.
Whatever the goddess decides, the people on the beach sing, dance, and welcome the new year.

On New Year's Eve, Cariocas gather on Rio's beaches to send offerings to Iemanjá, goddess of the sea.

WHEN THE WORLD TURNS UPSIDE DOWN

Because Brazil lies south of the equator, its summer begins in January. In February, at the hottest time of the year, the slow, steady throb of the *surdo* first sounds through the streets of Rio. The surdo is a huge bass drum that beats out the driving rhythm of the *samba*. And in Rio, the samba means Carnival.

Rio's Carnival is a riotous four-day celebration that leads up to Ash Wednesday. That is the beginning of Lent in the Roman Catholic calendar. Good Catholics are expected to give up worldly pleasures during Lent, the 40 days before Easter. The people of Rio prepare for this sober season by throwing an amazing blowout of a party. The samba is a wild, complex, dance. It sets the tone at Carnival time.

Rio's Carnival dancers wear elaborate, colorful costumes.

surdo (SOOR-DOO)
samba (SAHM-BAH)

Rio's Carnival is held in February, the hottest time of the year. That is when Cariocas put on colorful costumes and masks like this one to celebrate before the beginning of Lent.

Months before Carnival begins, elaborate costumes are designed and sewn and songs and dances are practiced to perfection. The time-consuming preparations are well worth it to the hardworking Cariocas. Carnival, after all, is the highlight of their year.

Preparations for Carnival begin months in advance. There are floats to design, costumes to sew, and songs and dances that must be practiced to perfection. Some of the poorest favelas

The Carnival dancer on the left represents the figure of a bull in a dance called the "Bumba Meu Bol."

The performers below are members of the Mangueira Samba School.

support *escolas de samba*, or samba schools. Each samba school creates a pageant for competition in the Carnival parade.

Carnival begins on the Saturday before Ash Wednesday. Hotels and private clubs host masquerade balls. They are attended by Rio's wealthiest citizens. Out in the streets, bands play and ordinary people turn out in extraordinary costumes. Everyone is pretending to be someone else. Beggars dress as kings and queens; men wear women's gowns; bankers and lawyers paint their faces like clowns. Food and drink, music and laughter are everywhere.

escolas de samba (ES-KOH-LAHS GEE SAHM-BAH)

The great *desfile*, or parade, starts on Sunday night. It lasts well into Monday afternoon. Some 80,000 people pack grandstands along Avenida Rio Branco and Avenida Presidente Vargas, two of the city's main thoroughfares. As many as forty samba schools present pageants. Each one lasts over an hour. Each samba school builds its pageant around a theme from Brazil's past. The floats and dances may tell the story of the Tamoio Indians or the first Portuguese explorers, the slave ships from Africa or the gold miners in the rain forest. But these pageants are not dry, schoolbook lessons on history. They are vibrant displays of color and

Left and below: Costumed Carnival participants

Opposite page: A samba school float in the Carnival parade

movement, woven together with the rhythms and lyrics of songs composed for this occasion.

A woman who works as a chambermaid or a boy who loads trucks at a warehouse must save for months to buy a Carnival costume. After a long day's work, they must rehearse for hours at the samba school for their parts in the pageant. Why do they do it? Their spirit is expressed in a popular Carnival song called *"O Primeiro Clarim"* ("The First Trumpet"): "Today, I don't want to suffer; Today, I don't want to cry . . . I want to be no one in the vast crowd."

desfile (DES-FEE-LEE)
Avenida Rio Branco (AH-VEH-NEE-dah HEE-OO BRAHN-KOO)
Avenida Presidente Vargas (AH-VEH-NEE-dah PREH-ZEE-DEHN-chee VAHR-gahz)
"O Primeiro Clarim" (OO PREE-MAY-ROO KLAH-REENGH)

PLAY BALL!

Cariocas love games. They set up volleyball nets on the beaches. When the sun is too hot, they go indoors to play billiards and table tennis. But the city's true passion is *futebol*, the game Americans know as soccer.

Sometime around 1900, Charles Miller, a Brazilian of British descent, went to England to attend a university. There, he fell in love with the game of soccer. When he returned to Brazil, he taught the game to his friends. It caught on quickly. In 1906, the Rio Football League was established.

British soccer emphasized toughness, strength, and a fierce team spirit. In Rio, the game soon took on a tropical flavor. Cariocas play a brand of soccer noted for grace, speed, and style. Typical moves have such colorful names as the banana kick, the overhead backward bicycle kick, and the back-of-the-heels flip-on.

People play soccer all over Rio. Schools, factories, and favelas sponsor their own teams. But major-league competitions take place in the city's vast Maracanã Stadium. It is the largest outdoor soccer field in the world. It can hold 180,000 people. Spectators become wildly excited during soccer matches. To keep them from rushing out among the players, the field at Maracanã Stadium is surrounded by a deep moat.

Rio's enthusiasm for soccer builds to an exciting climax every four years. That is when the World Cup Soccer Championship games are played. Time after time, Brazil has produced leading teams. The world's most famous soccer player is known to his adoring fans as Pelé. Pelé grew up in a small Brazilian town but became Rio's hero. Born Edson Arantes do Nascimento, Pelé led Brazil to World Cup championships in 1958, 1962, and 1970.

These volleyball players on Ipanema Beach have a great view of Dois Irmãos Peak.

Dois Irmãos (DOYZ EEHR-MOWZ)

Capoeira

Slaves who came to Rio from present-day Angola brought a form of martial art called *capoeira*. The opponents circled around one another, attacking with graceful, lightning-swift kicks. Because slaves were forbidden to fight, capoeira was disguised as a ritual dance. It survives today as a dance, a performance for tourists, and a martial art. Its parries, feints, and high kicks call for incredible flexibility rather than brute strength.

Streamers are everywhere during this soccer game in Maracanã Stadium.

futebol (FOO-CHEE-BAHWL)
Maracanã (MAH-RAH-KAH-NANH)
Pelé (PEH-LEH)
Edson Arantes do Nascimento (EH-GEE-SOHN AH-RAHN-CHEES DOO NAH-SEE-MENGH-TOO)
capoeira (KAH-POO-AY-RAH)

At Carnival time, Cariocas sing a song called *"Cidade Maravilhosa."* The title translates as "Marvelous City" or "City of Wonders." Among all of the world's cities, Rio is unique. Beyond its civilized parks and gardens, it contains steep mountains and untamed rain forests. Its endless beaches are a glorious playground for young and old. Nestled among glass-and-steel towers are houses and cathedrals that recall nearly 500 years of history.

"Cidade Maravilhosa" (SEE-DAH-GEE MAH-RAH-VEE-LYOH-SAH)

PLACES TO REMEMBER

Rio's neighborhoods are linked by a network of bus lines and a subway system. Nevertheless, the automobile rules the streets. Cariocas drive with the same wild abandon they throw into Carnival. They careen around corners and hurtle through red lights. Shattered lightpoles and smashed vehicles with their wheels in the air are everyday sights. About 2,000 people a year die in traffic accidents. This means that, on average, automobiles kill people in Rio at the rate of one every three hours. Visitors must be very careful when crossing the streets to explore the unforgettable sights of Rio.

The Native Americans who once lived around Guanabara Bay were driven into the rain forest by the European settlers. Their history and traditions are preserved in the Museu do Indio, the Indian Museum, on Rua das Palmeiras. Life-sized portraits of today's Indian families adorn the walls. Scattered among them are paintings of native peoples by some of the first Europeans who reached Brazil's shores.

An evening view of Sugarloaf Mountain

This graceful pink-and-white building in Rio is surrounded by lovely trees and gardens.

Other displays include magnificent feather headdresses made from the colorful plumage of Brazil's tropical birds. Some are towering crowns. Others cover the hair and cascade over the shoulders in flowing waves of green, orange, red, and blue. Photographs and films capture the music, dance, and customs of Brazil's native peoples.

On nearby Rua São Clemente stands the Casa Rui Barbosa. That is the mansion where Brazil's first constitution was written in 1889. The splendid furniture and the elaborate salons and dining rooms are reminders of the way Rio's aristocracy once lived.

Museu do Indio (MOO-ZEH-OO DOO EENE-GEE-OO)
Rua das Palmeiras (HOO-AH DAHS PAHL-MAY-RAHS)
Rua São Clemente (HOO-AH SOW KLEH-MAYN-CHEE)
Casa Rui Barbosa (KAH-SAH HOO-EE BAR-BOH-ZAH)

Built in the eighteenth century, the Gloria Church was favored by Brazil's imperial family. According to legend, a hermit once lived in a hut on this site. In 1671, two angels supposedly visited him and helped him carve an exquisite statue of Our Lady of Glory. For seventeen years, pilgrims traveled to see this wonder. It was said to cure the sick who prayed before it. At last, the hermit returned to Portugal, taking the statue with him. On the way, his ship went down in a storm. Miraculously, the statue washed up on a Portuguese beach. A replica stands in the Gloria Church today, but the original remains in Portugal.

King João VI was responsible for Rio's beautiful Botanical Garden, shown here.

Venus's-flytraps (right) grow in a greenhouse at the Botanical Garden.

Bougainvillea blooms (below) make a striking splash of color.

King João VI was determined to refine life in the wild Brazilian colony. His handiwork can still be seen in Rio's beautiful Botanical Garden on Rua Jardim Botânico. The garden contains more than 135,000 plants and trees—900 varieties of palm tree alone. Among the garden's most spectacular attractions are giant Victoria Regia water lilies measuring 21 feet around. A greenhouse holds a collection of Venus's-flytraps and other insect-eating plants. The Avenue of Palms is a stunning promenade beneath an arched canopy of palm fronds.

Rua Jardim Botânico (HOO-AH ZHAR-GEENGH BOH-TANGH-NEE-KOO)

ON THE WILD SIDE

From north to south, Rio is fringed by natural beaches. Most of them swarm with human visitors. The sand bristles with umbrellas, volleyball nets, and bathhouses. Yet, tame though they seem, the beaches are pounded by fierce Atlantic breakers. Any swimmer who ventures into the surf will be awed by the ocean's crashing force. The people of Rio can never forget the power, harshness, and abundance of nature.

Rio's beautiful beaches look peaceful, but they are pounded by the Atlantic Ocean's crashing breakers.

Because the crashing waves can be so dangerous, most Cariocas who visit the beaches stay very near the shore in the shallowest water—if they venture into the water at all!

This Copacabana shrimp vendor sells his wares to beachgoers in need of a snack.

The Floresta da Tijuca rain forest, within Rio's city limits, has been preserved as a national park.

The caiman pictured below is similar to an alligator. Because the rain forest is protected, animals that live there are safe from hunters.

Throughout the year, plant life flourishes in Rio's tropical climate. Within the city's limits sprawls the Floresta da Tijuca rain forest. It is 100 square miles of wilderness preserved as a national park. Here, within earshot of the city's traffic, lies a world of tall, straight trees. Their leafy, matted branches form a dense canopy high above the ground. Snakelike vines swing earthward, and stunning orchids cling to the tree trunks. Giant bougainvilleas, begonias, passionflowers, and other blossoms splash the forest with color.

Monkeys and scarlet macaws are among the amazing variety of animals and birds that live in the Floresta da Tijuca.

From the canopy overhead, monkeys shriek and fling twigs at unwary visitors. The canopy is also home to possums, raccoons, and a mischievous furry creature called the coatimundi.

On the ground, armadillos and anteaters trundle along through the fallen leaves. The rain forest is loud with birdsong, especially at dawn and sundown. The dense foliage harbors some of the world's most poisonous snakes, and the air hums with insects day and night.

Floresta da Tijuca (FLOH-REHS-TAH DEH CHEE-ZHOO-KAH)

The city of Rio nestles at the foot of the great Serra do Mar mountain chain, which stretches for 1,500 miles along the Brazilian coast. Jagged peaks and mountain spurs extend into the city itself, destroying any hope that its streets could follow a gridlike pattern. The mountains break the city into two parts—the long, narrow South Zone of beaches and hotels, and the city center and the North Zone around Guanabara Bay. The Portuguese sailors who first saw Rio's mountains gave them the colorful

The jagged peaks and mountain spurs of the Serra do Mar chain break Rio into two parts—the South Zone and the North Zone.

The early Portuguese sailors gave Sugarloaf Mountain (visible in the background) its name.

names they carry to this day: Pão de Açucar (Sugarloaf), Corcovado (Hunchback), Arpoador (Harpooner), Dois Irmãos (Two Brothers), and Gávea (Topsail). Rio's streets twist up, down, and around these mountains in a hopelessly bewildering tangle.

A night view of Rio from the top of Sugarloaf

Serra do Mar (SEH-HAH DOO MAHR)
Pão de Açucar (POW GEE AH-SOO-KAHR)
Arpoador (AHR-POO-AH-DOR)
Gávea (GAH-VEE-AH)

53

Pão de Açucar, or Sugarloaf, is the subject of one of the most popular postcard pictures of Rio. The mountain seems to soar straight upward, as though its sides were sheer cliffs. Throughout the year, cable cars carry visitors to the summit, which offers a splendid view of the city below.

A cable car carrying visitors to the top of Sugarloaf Mountain

This beautiful aerial view of Sugarloaf makes it clear why the mountain is such a popular subject for postcard pictures.

The view of Rio from the granite peak of Corcovado is truly the most beautiful. Below, the city spreads in a rich panorama—its gently curving beaches, its hills and highways, the blue waters of Guanabara Bay. From this height, Rio's skyscrapers look like toy towers dotting the magnificent natural landscape.

At the crown of Corcovado, Christ the Redeemer stands alone. The figure's great arms stretch wide in blessing over the crowded streets of Rio de Janeiro.

A beautiful view of the city of Rio de Janeiro

Luiz de Abreu Vieira e Silva
(LOO-EEZ GEE AH-BREH-OO VEE-AY-RAH EE SEEL-VAH)

Brazilian Spices

Many of the spices grown in Rio's gardens today were brought to Brazil by a Portuguese adventurer named Luiz de Abreu Vieira e Silva. While he was a prisoner of the French in the East Indies, he managed to fill his pockets with seeds from a large spice garden. When he finally made a daring escape, he carried his treasure to Brazil. Much of the cinnamon, nutmeg, clove, and avocado that grows in Rio today descended from the seeds Vieira e Silva stole from his French captors long ago.

FAMOUS LANDMARKS

Between Copacabana Beach and Avenue Atlântica is "Copa Walk," a wide sidewalk with a distinctive mosaic wave pattern.

Ipanema Beach

Sugarloaf Mountain

The Praça Mauá
The 17th-century monastery of São Bento stands just off this square. It contains many master-pieces of colonial painting and sculpture.

Copacabana Beach
Copacabana is the heart of Rio's resort district. A magnet for tourists, it is flanked by the city's most elegant hotels.

Ipanema Beach
This beach is somewhat less crowded than Copacabana. It attracts a younger crowd, as well as musicians and joggers.

Sugarloaf Mountain
A steep, flat-topped mountain at the entrance to Guanabara Bay, Sugarloaf stands 1,325 feet tall. Two cogwheel trains carry visitors to the summit for a stunning view of the city.

Corcovado
This mountain is crowned with the famous statue of Christ the Redeemer. The 700-ton statue, completed in 1931, was built with money raised by churches throughout Brazil.

Paquetá Island
The most picturesque of the 84 islands that dot Guanabara Bay, it can be reached only by boat. It is the home of about 3,000 people, mostly fishermen.

Floresta da Tijuca
This tropical forest preserve is only a 20-minute ride from down-town Rio. Along its winding paths, visitors can see orchids, parrots, and monkeys.

A lovely waterfall in the
Floresta da Tijuca rain forest

*Corcovado Mountain is
crowned with the famous
statue of Christ the Reedemer.*

Largo da Carioca (Carioca Square)
This concrete plaza in central Rio is crowded with street vendors, musicians, and spiritist healers.

Catedral Metropolitana (Metropolitan Cathedral)
Noted for its enormous stained-glass windows, this cathedral is the favorite church of Rio's elite. It was formerly known as the Royal Chapel.

Avenida Rio Branco
One of Rio's main thoroughfares, this bustling street was once lined with elegant restaurants and shops. It is now a very commercial street.

Teatro Municipal (Municipal Theater)
Brazil's leading theater building, it is modeled on the Paris Opera House. Opened in 1909, it features opera, ballet, and concerts. Its distinctive bronze roof is crowned by a sculpted eagle.

Paço Imperial (Imperial Palace)
Once the emperor's administrative offices, this lovely building was fully restored in 1985. The museum hosts shifting exhibits about Brazil's history.

Museu Nacional (National Museum)
Housed in the former home of the emperors, this museum displays Indian artifacts and specimens of the region's minerals, plants, and butterflies.

FAST FACTS

POPULATION   1994

City: 5,093,232

Metropolitan Area: 9,800,000

Rio de Janeiro is the 2nd-largest city in Brazil. Only São Paulo has more people.

AREA 452 square miles

CLIMATE Rio is a humid, tropical city. It has sunny days all year round. In July, the average temperature is 68 degrees Fahrenheit. In February (Rio's summer), the average is 79 degrees Fahrenheit. Annual rainfall averages 44 inches. Rain is heaviest in Rio's summer season, from January through March.

ECONOMY Factories in Rio produce about 10 percent of Brazil's industrial output. The city manufactures processed foods, chemicals, pharmaceuticals, and metals. Rio is also the home of many of the nation's leading banks, and of the leading Brazilian stock market. Rio has long been a center for trade and has extensive shipyards. Highways and railways link it with other cities in South America.

CHRONOLOGY

1500
Pedro Alvares Cabral, a Portuguese captain, is the first European to set foot on Brazilian soil.

1502
A Portuguese expedition reaches the shores of Guanabara Bay on January 1. Thinking the bay is the mouth of a wide river, the Portuguese name the place *Rio de Janeiro* (River of January).

1565
Estácio de Sá establishes a military outpost on Guanabara Bay. He calls the spot São Sebastião do Rio de Janeiro, the city's official name today.

1567
Estácio de Sá leads a successful attack on the French settlement at Guanabara Bay. Rio and the surrounding area are in Portuguese hands.

1800
People of African descent outnumber Europeans in Rio.

Passengers who can't fit inside this crowded trolley find a way to get where they want to go.

1807
Fleeing Napoleon Bonaparte, Prince Regent Dom João of Portugal (later King João VI) sets up the royal court in Rio.

1822
Pedro I declares Brazil independent from Portugal, with himself as its emperor.

1840
Pedro II takes the throne at the Imperial Palace in Rio, beginning Brazil's golden age.

1888
Princess Isabel signs the *Lei Aurea* (Golden Law), freeing the slaves of Brazil.

1889
Pedro II is overthrown; Brazil becomes a republic.

1931
The statue of Jesus Christ the Redeemer is erected on the peak of Corcovado.

1960
Brasília replaces Rio as capital of Brazil.

1994
Brazil wins the World Cup Soccer Championship for the fourth time in its history.

RIO DE JANEIRO

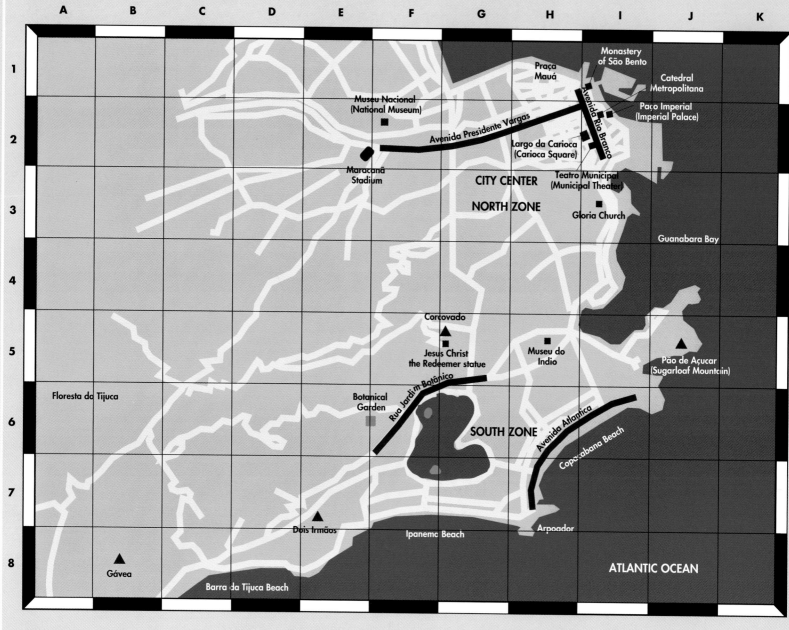

Arpoador	H7	
Atlantic Ocean	C,D,E,F,G,H,I 8	
Avenida Atlantica	H,I 6	
Avenida Presidente Vargas	F,G,H 2	
Avenida Rio Branco	H,I 1,2	

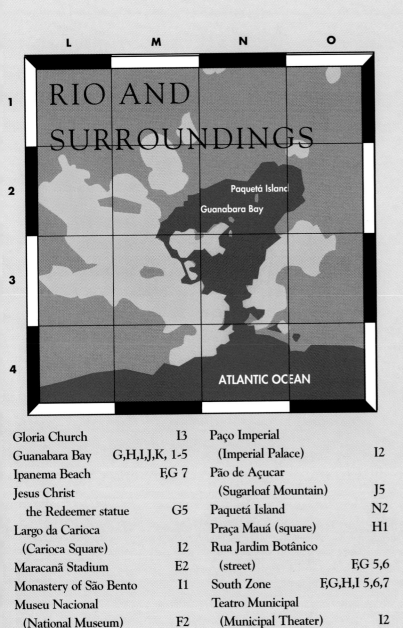

L   M   N   O

1
RIO AND
SURROUNDINGS

2
Paquetá Island
Guanabara Bay

3

4
ATLANTIC OCEAN

Gloria Church	I3	Paço Imperial	
Guanabara Bay	G,H,I,J,K, 1-5	(Imperial Palace)	I2
Ipanema Beach	F,G 7	Pão de Açucar	
Jesus Christ		(Sugarloaf Mountain)	J5
the Redeemer statue	G5	Paquetá Island	N2
Largo da Carioca		Praça Mauá (square)	H1
(Carioca Square)	I2	Rua Jardim Botânico	
Maracanã Stadium	E2	(street)	F,G 5,6
Monastery of São Bento	I1	South Zone	F,G,H,I 5,6,7
Museu Nacional		Teatro Municipal	
(National Museum)	F2	(Municipal Theater)	I2
Museu do Indio	H5		

GLOSSARY

abolish: Do away with; forbid

blighted: Declining; decaying; destroyed

cogwheel train: Locomotive specially designed for climbing steep slopes; its "cogwheel" has teeth that lock with teeth along a central rail to keep the train from slipping backward

exquisite: Beautiful; delicate; very lovely

convert: To change a person's belief from one religion to another

favela: Shantytown built on a hillside in Brazil

lithe: Supple; limber

medium: Person thought to have the power to communicate with the spirits of the dead

moat: Deep ditch, sometimes filled with water, surrounding a castle or a field

mosaic: Picture or design made by setting small colored pieces of tile or another material into mortar

mulato: Person of mixed African and European ancestry in Brazil

pageant: Elaborate dramatic representation depicting some historical or traditional event

prince regent: Prince who rules when the sovereign is unavailable

replica: Exact copy

throng: Crowd; a large number

unique: One-of-a kind

unwary: Careless; not cautious

vast: Covering a very large area; huge; tremendous

Picture Identifications

Cover: A green-winged macaw; carnival beads; a Rio beach lined with condos and hotels; Brazilian woman
Page 1: Men playing beach volleyball
Pages 4-5: An aerial view of Rio
Pages 8-9: A Carnival dancer
Pages 20-21: An eighteenth-century depiction of Rio de Janeiro (São Sebastião do Rio de Janeiro)
Pages 30-31: Floats in the Carnival parade
Pages 42-43: A Rio beach lined with condos and hotels

Photo Credits

Cover: (top left) ©Robert Fried; cover (background), ©Ondas Press/**Rex Interstock Ltd.**; cover (carnival beads), ©**KK&A, Ltd.**; cover (bottom right), ©Robert Fried;1, ©Donald Nausbaum/**Tony Stone Images, Inc.**; 3, ©**KK&A, Ltd.**; 4-5, ©B. Bachmann/Camerique/**H. Armstrong Roberts**; 6 (left), ©SuperStock International, Inc.; 6 (right), ©Thierry Cazabon/**Tony Stone Images, Inc.**; 7, ©Manfred Gottschalk/**Tom Stack & Associates**; 8-9, ©Tony Morrison/**South American Pictures**; 10, ©**Robert Fried**; 11 (top), ©**Robert Fried**; 11 (bottom), ©Sue Cunningham/**Tony Stone Images, Inc.**; 12 (cardboard), ©**KK&A, Ltd.**; 12 (bottom), ©**Robert Fried**; 13 (top), ©Sue Cunningham/**Tony Stone Images, Inc.**; 13 (bottom), ©Tony Morrison/**South American Pictures**; 14, ©**Robert Fried**; 15 (both pictures), ©**Robert Fried**; 16, ©L. Potter/**Camerique/H. Armstrong Roberts**; 17 (top), ©Tony Morrison/**South American Pictures**; 17 (bottom), ©**Photri, Inc.**;18 (both pictures), ©**Robert Fried**; 19 (top), ©**Robert Fried**; 19 (candles), ©**KK&A, Ltd.**; 20-21, **North Wind Picture Archives**; 22, **Universidade Estadual de Campinas, Biblioteca Centrál**; 23 (both pictures), **Universidade Estadual de Campinas, Biblioteca Centrál**; 24, **Stock Montage, Inc.**; 25 (top), **Stock Montage, Inc.**; 25 (bottom), **The Bettmann Archive**; 26 (left), **Universidade Estadual de Campinas, Biblioteca Centrál**; 26-27, **Stock Montage, Inc.**; 27 (top right), **Universidade Estadual de Campinas, Biblioteca Centrál**; 27 (coffee beans), ©**KK&A, Ltd.**; 28, ©Daren Bell/**Rex Interstock Ltd.**; 29 (top), ©Steve Vidler/**SuperStock International, Inc.**; 29 (both bottom pictures), **UPI/Bettmann**; 30-31, ©John Starr/**Tony Stone Images, Inc.**; 32 (ribbons and lipstick), ©**KK&A, Ltd.**; 32-33, ©Woody Woodworth/**SuperStock International, Inc.**; 34, ©Ary Diesendruck/**Tony Stone Images, Inc.**; 35 (top), ©R. Kord/**H. Armstrong Roberts**; 35 (Carnival mask), ©**KK&A, Ltd.**; 36 (left), ©Interstock/Bavaria/**H. Armstrong Roberts**; 36 (right), ©**Robert Fried**; 37 (left), ©**Robert Fried**; 37 (right), ©Tony Morrison/**South American Pictures**; 38 (beads), ©**KK&A, Ltd.**; 38 (both pictures), ©**Cameramann International, Ltd.**; 39, ©Ary Diesendruck/**Tony Stone Images, Inc.**; 40, ©Jeff Greenberg/**Unicorn Stock Photos**; 41 (top left), ©Tony Morrison/**South American Pictures**; 41 (top right), ©**Robert Fried**; 41 (soccer shoe), ©**KK&A, Ltd.**; 42-43, ©Ondas Press/**Rex Interstock Ltd.**; 44, ©Manfred Gottschalk/**Tom Stack & Associates**; 45 (left), ©**Robert Fried**; 45 (right), ©Kennon Cooke/**Valan Photos**; 46, ©**Robert Fried**; 47 (top), ©Prof. R.C. Simpson/**Valan Photos**; 47 (bottom), ©Kennon Cooke/**Valan Photos**; 48, ©**Tony Stone Images, Inc.**; 49 (top), ©**Tony Stone Images, Inc.**; 49 (bottom left), ©**Robert Fried**; 49 (bottom right), ©Jeff Greenberg/**Unicorn Stock Photos**; 50 (top), ©Tony Morrison/**South American Pictures**; 50 (bottom), ©**Robert Fried**; 51 (top), ©**Robert Fried**; 51 (bottom), ©John Cancalosi/**Valan Photos**; 52, ©Pascal Rondeau/**Tony Stone Images, Inc.**; 53 (top), ©ZEFA/**H. Armstrong Roberts**; 53 (bottom), ©Jean-Marie Jro/**Valan Photos**; 54 (top), ©Karl Kummels/**SuperStock International, Inc.**; 54 (bottom), ©Manfred Gottschalk/**Tom Stack & Associates**; 55 (top), ©ZEFA/**H. Armstrong Roberts**; 55 (spices), ©**KK&A, Ltd.**; 56 (left), ©Bill Bachmann/**Photo Edit**; 56 (middle), ©R. Kord/**H. Armstrong Roberts**; 56 (right), ©Jeff Greenberg/**Unicorn Stock Photos**; 57 (left), ©**Photri, Inc.**; 57 (right), ©R. Kord/**H. Armstrong Roberts**; 59, ©**Photri, Inc.**; 60 & 61, ©**KK&A, Ltd.**

INDEX

Page numbers in boldface type indicate illustrations

ABOUT THE AUTHOR

Deborah Kent grew up in Little Falls, New Jersey, and received her B.A. in English from Oberlin College. She earned an M.A. in Social Work from the Smith College of Social Work, and worked for several years at the University Settlement House in New York City. For five years she lived in San Miguel de Allende, Mexico, where she wrote her first novel for young adults. Deborah Kent is the author of a dozen young-adult novels as well as many titles in the Childrens Press America the Beautiful series. She lives in Chicago with her husband and their daughter Janna.